Screams from a Barb-wired Room

by littledeadboy

INTRODUCTION

Welcome to my twisted little world. My name is David Goodrum, but you might also know me by my Twitter name, littledeadboy. I've written poetry much of my life, but I didn't discover the real power of words until I was 15. That's when I consider myself to have truly started writing poetry, and indeed, I've never stopped since then nor will I ever.

What you have before you is a collection of some of the best poems I wrote while I was still in high school. I didn't include very many from early on because I needed much more practice still, and throughout this book the style of this poetic pandemonium changes significantly. The very first poem is a revised version of the poem that "woke me up" to the true power of art.

Over the course of time these poems were written, I went through incredible personal changes. Early on I was very naive and knew very little of the true nature of reality and the world I lived in. By the end of the book when I had reached age 18, however, I had finally expanded this awareness significantly, although I still had a long way to go. I still wasn't totally "grown up," and in some ways I never will inasmuch as that equates to accepting the status quo. But at the time of writing this I am much more mature.

My political views during this time were extremely leftist. I was basically a Socialist or even a Communist, although I was also very much a Libertarian, almost, perhaps, Anarchist. I didn't actually start learning much of anything about politics until late 2006, when I came upon many leftist ideas, writers, artists, etc. My political views did slowly change throughout the book, however they are now quite different. I'm not sure they can be accurately classified as anything within the political spectrum, but the closest thing I come to is a Libertarian. I do not support anarchy, and I am against Socialism.

And of course, I must now bring up religion. During the early days of this book, I was technically a Christian, though not much of a practicing one. Indeed, if any fundamentalist Christians read some of what you are about to read, they would shriek in horror proclaiming words like this could only come "from the Devil." Perhaps, in a sense, they did. In April of 2006, my tenth grade year, I at last started to think critically about religion. After mulling it over for about a week, I decided I did not in fact believe in God, at least not one described by any religion.

But in 2006, I came upon some very dark information. Some of the people I mentioned earlier with the leftist politics were not just pro-Socialism, they were basically Luciferians. By the end of my eleventh grade year I had read much of Aleister Crowley's Liber al vel Legis, or The Book of the Law, and for a short time was more or less a Thelemite. It's hard for me to remember how long this lasted. While my mind always remained open, for a period of time I will admit, unfortunately, I was a bit brainwashed and deceived by "the dark side," although I always had the best of intentions. As I paved the road to proverbial Hell. But that's life. I have no religion now. I just believe what I believe, and it doesn't include any of these "dark" things, at least not in my opinion.

Oh. Also, something else everyone likes to focus on. I am gay, 100% homosexual, as people who dare to read this book will undoubtedly discover soon into it. I am definitely not your typical homosexual, if there is such a thing. It is a part of my experience in this reality, but there is really so much more to me than that.

Much of this book is extremely dark. My dark poetry often ends up being my best, but there are also poems that explore other frequencies in these pages. During these extremely dark times of my life, I often hoped I could one day expose to the world the indescribable level of suffering I experienced that I expressed in words. Ultimately, it is a story of survival, a tapestry of the struggle of existence faced by humanity since the dawn of humankind. At least, during most of recorded history. The message is I survived everything in this book. Thus the message, overall, is a positive one. Enjoy the feast.

"Run if you can, walk if you have to, crawl if you must, just never give up." - Dean Karnazes

The Revelation

Living again
Feeling too familiar
Forgetting the end
A 7-time lobotomized blur

Pain of disbelief
Within this darkness of worms
I'm not there, and I don't want to be here
Come watch me find my terms

The undying connection
The misinterpretation of civilization
The failure to understand could take me
Away to the self-providing vegetable world of insanity
There I will run in the open wilderness of night
Running and hiding and searching for the one who will fight the parasite
With burning tears behind my eyes...

Held within
Refusing to sin
Behold the one I want to taste
Doing it once again…

September 2, 2005
[edited August 29, 2010]

The Fiends

Fucking infection
My mistakes…
Some kind of redemption… no protection…
Those dead days… DEAD days…
Like I ruined… (no)…
Sick
Definite hypocrite

Remember me, enemy?
You made me afraid
You flourished while I decayed
Everyone said I was dead
Wandering like ghosts through my head
Your punishment found in flames
…
I'm sorry, my love; pay no attention to them
They are what remain from a past that is dead
(No...we can be together...it doesn't matter what they think)
…EFFING ES OH BEES
RUINING EVERYTHING!
I call upon the ancient spirits
Shouting my cry
Time for vindication… time for vengeance…
NOW YOU FEAR IT
…
(No… it's not right) I can't believe what I was forced to do
From a mind desperately needing to find you
(I only wanted to be confronted)
I dreamed… in the presence of the fiends
…I will fright the parasite with delight tonight…

You're always lying… I'm always defying
No protection from the infection
It was deception
Boundaries of words…
Relative concepts through what recurs

When I see my enemy, my vision blurs…
Like a devil
I wanna choke his throat
Crying to torture…

I become the Holy Creature
Destined to fight the Ultimate Deceiver

Take a step back… take a step back…
I need these words to reverse the curse of the worst possible thirst
Sometimes I like to repeat it… verse by verse…

A scavenger for truth
Its impurity
Is for me
Not for you

November 6, 2005
[edited August 29, 2010]

Winter Warrior

Searching through the trees
Today there is no breeze
Residual hauntings resonate here
Desecrated by disgraces who never tasted fear

Hunting through the snow
For things I may never know
Seeing your stride in my mind
Walking free for all time

Come see my thoughts
Memories you awakened
Not one time you fought
Will ever be forsaken

November 29, 2005
[edited September 9, 2010]

i[lluminati]Pod

Enter into… an obscure world
I'm inside the screen that is seen with the eye…
I am the pod
I am i
And I can see you right through…my view
As I wait for you…to watch me…watch me

And I'm waiting…
I'm creating…
For you…

Take me to school
Every day, your…slave
And I won't be a fool…and I won't be afraid

You betrayed
Play me now
Insert your dirty movie…of purity
Like silk from a spider…and I'm filthy
I'll be it – you'll see it
You carry me around
Until you want to hear my sound
I once did too…
When instead I should have seen the real
Let's play your games
I hear whispered names

You cannot rest…
I'm still waiting…
In the blackness of your pocket
I am practicing
Here in this warm, dark place

I heard you

December 31, 2005
[edited August 29, 2010]

Ice Prison

Dark clouds every day
This one remains the same
It's not that I still feel betrayed
I just couldn't find the light's way

And now I feel dependent
Packages of pain are sent in
I wish this life to one day end
With he as my only friend...

You could be all I know
And together we could go
Far away from this place of pain
We could hold on to each other
And never look back again
But this is the horrible real world

Struggling to see
Your place...for me
It can be so hard to perceive
When the truth is hard to believe

But I still remember
Your serene purity, back in September
We didn't have to care, it was just you and me
The existence of death was to never be

I'm right by you
I fight to do
Something to save us once more
I'm screaming inside
But I too have to hide
I wish I could show you the truth
You're the one I'm fighting for

Now it's time to leave
I know you're the first to go
I'm sorry I couldn't offer relief
In this hellish time of sorrow
So our pain brings this rain
Killing beauty of the snow

…it should be easy
but we're prisoners
of this reality...

January 3, 2006
[edited August 29, 2010]

Whispers

Silent
tired
solitude
I heard the perpetual pitch
of his laughter...
I'll remember forever
Sitting, staying
all alone
Eyes closing
on my own?
I can't stop
Myself...anymore
Everyday
I listen
Wanting
hurting
more

February 6, 2006
[edited September 14, 2010]

Unfed

Getting fed
With dancing demonic memories in my head
Their flame, their cry
Used when the secret tried to get through
Sitting there… just being…
Listening to a stranger speaking
The words enter my mind like darkness light must find
There's no stopping…this talking
Polluted like a revolution
No way out… obliged to observe the wild words of infection

Fed and fueled by prophecies
I still sense these bloody things…churning…
While I'm learning, listening to
the public secrets
I wish I could return
with what I've learned
Back to that past
spreading my disease ever so fast

Look out the window
See the snow
And my poem
Becomes a rainbow
Liquid decay – cause for delay
Schooled and controlled by the same suckling source…
Instructed upon what to do
by a non-human force

…yesterday we uniquely united,
today…we display the super psychosis
…until the secret is ignited…

February 9, 2006
[edited August 29, 2010]

Dark Light

In these days of disease
I begin to see things
In a dark light
Like a smile of betrayal
A cold void of a voice
Trying to sound gentle…
As it speaks to the one… I love…
…about something so… impertinent, unimportant
Completely insignificant…to the words' true purpose…
He tried
Back in the day when he could
And I…uncertain
…sat too still for my reaction
…I have to care…
No choice exists
I cannot change
I can only continue to persist
Every day it runs through my mind
Like the wild one I have yet to find
…so wild and free…
just how I'd be
I cannot like when it comes to the kill
How can I fight if I cannot feel?
This world isn't real…
My world isn't real…

February 12, 2006
[edited August 29, 2010]

Artifacts

I sit there, in my room
And look over... and see...
the same game
I look in an old book...
the same name
I imagine
the same play
They are remnants of missed moments
Tangible memories of lost days

February 23, 2006
[edited September 16, 2010]

His Words

Entwined in
deception…

I heard his words
they burned every nerve
So tell me…did he have
prickly…skin?
Upon the liberation
of potential lies, did it hurt
did it burn in his eyes?

This could be the end…
Everything I ever knew…
To never see the innocent days again
And no longer be a part of you…

All those days of purity and games
The true one I knew you to be
I still never knew of the unafraid
You still don't know what you meant to me

Now we're older – life is darker
I'm left in a lonely void of inactivity
But the pure one you were in the past
is still the one I see

Now you have left
So I am dead
No way will math explain
my exponential regret
So as you live your life
Testing me by talking
Please consider…
I'm always listening

I'm left lurking in a limbo world
The lack, the vacancy, of any real veracity
Eternally lonely, like a stone secured beneath rocks,
beneath stars, bearing scars, so internal, so emotional,
with no way, to find a place, for the pain

Like a curtain of uncertain
Drawn upon my mind's eyes
No divinity can reveal to me the eventuality
The longed-for unleashing of the Infinite I

February 28, 2006
[edited August 30, 2010]

Under the Capstone

Under control
Watching me
an eye of slavery
Receiving secrets
like an illegal police frequency
Pertinent
to all these...heretic memories
inside me...

Sick with the disease, heart beating
so full from feeding...
Dining upon demon spawn
Killing colonies of parasites
crawling towards me
as I'm gorging
Haunted by the horrors of Horus
hunted by werewolves
in a thick and twisted
forest
burning
embodiments of creation
I cringe to remember
to be forgetful is futile
defilement
of everything I ever meant

March 6, 2006
[edited September 16, 2010]

Mutation

I saw him once again
In these rotting days of death
leading up to the end

Waiting for anything
Satisfied with even senseless salvation
Betraying him for nothing
So becomes my care for creation…
…

It's time to review
…no…What did you do?!
You wrote your way away –
you lived to die another day

Do these words
come with a curse?

Will you be afraid,
and stop before you create?
…crazed creations of heresy…
Crazed Creations of Heresy

I will…still…
be me…
Here, in all agony
There's no such thing as free

So collect the debt
of everything you ever said

Wait. This is a strange mutation
of the hidden, lone chromosome
I suppose I need

to kill what I kill…

Make your choice...
bring out your voice
seize the disease

He formulates lies
to catalyze my demise

I've been freed to feed
plant the poetic seed
It stems from personal need

It doesn't matter anymore
I search, I find more

I have become so powerful...
I AM UNSTOPPABLE...

YOU TRY TO SLAY ME
I DECREE DECAY
YOU BLEED
ENDLESSLY

I join forces with the voices
To power more poetry
We are the soldiers...

WE...ARE...PAIN KILLERS

March 15, 2006
[edited August 30, 2010]

2

Same place
Same disgrace
Same face
Same dead fate

(2 years)
Full of the future
Death by desire
(2 fears)
No light, no hope, no safety
(100,000 unshed tears)

my world decays, the one betrays
moved by movies + music
(forget me, betray me… but you don't know)
Afraid, lonely…
secretly..............
Save me!

March 27, 2006
[edited August 31, 2010]

Crypt

The onset of…the strange pain
It is unidentified…
But that doesn't matter… I won't
wait all day and all night
Like the gesticulation of a parasite
Like the gestation of a mummy…
deep down, in some darkened crypt
it slipped…into a prominent pyramid
my pyramid of pain…
crawling onward, doing…homework
it hurts, it curses…me
like an ancient spell, a witch of sorrow
i encounter…similar power…
to fight…morning, day, or night
…any time…in my life
behold, I've located the secret
the way to remain…able…to write

March 30, 2006
[edited August 30, 2010]

The Boy

he's the boy i knew
from long ago
the moment i see him...
i become as softly frozen as snow

sitting there, in the car
i watch and wonder
if he, so close yet far,
is doing as i have done
...

these days feel empty,
i no longer understand the meaning
but he's the one i keep seeing
i've lost all he knew
he's lost all I know
i only know what i want to do...

If he could just be
with me tomorrow
I'd no longer be
a slave to sorrow
I would show him such amazing things
I would bring forth the love lost in
all my poetic singing

But just to see him as I did there
About nothing else could I care
Give me the strength to unleash the secret
Before the end...a pleasant experience

April 4, 2006
[edited August 31, 2010]

Room of Glass

everything slowly changing…
reduced to regretful nothing
it's our status, our…relationship
…dying… non-existent

every day contains
another episodic nightmare
the profound prickly pain,
the horror I overhear

and i can…feel…the end
coming closer…cuffed to cut
and he can't perceive
any of my misery, accurately
so i try to survive
but i can't in that…class
i become so nervous
like the room is glass
and it's hungry to break
like me, it wants to be
freed at last, and I cannot take
the sharp shards as they cut my lip
like everything he will ever say
and every word he ever said…

…i am the corrupt
i'm different
i've become the other one
oh…how i didn't

now step into the room
a jail cell built in Hell
you can smell the fumes
on a rail of radiation
it…fills my lungs…
inside suffocation,

outside sophistication
i'm done and the residue
formulates into… a
hopeless …irritation…

i stand like a man
ready to defeat the beast
but no one understands
what I need

…no (can't you stop? must you continue? …no…)
this is so close to the breaking point…

i don't even feel the pain anymore…
just a single tingly numb horror
at home, i can go to places
of great magic, but they
are not real…
…& neither is the great prophecy……
(I take more lies.)

April 11, 2006
[edited August 31, 2010]

Red Sun Misery

…i feel i've been
resurrected to die again…
…i feel…this is
finally the end…

Enter betrayal…
a certain innocence, held in
dying essence…the flavor
which, is better bitter
I stood there again, listening
with intent
Like a warped addict wanting
his fix…and there's plenty of it

The one had some fun
in a world without me
Something disgusting to her, or intriguing to he
- the great perpetual purity, crazy… CRAZY!
I heard him more
Like horror
This time
Did he…
dine on sunshine?

sexually suggestive, red-alert revelation
kept from me

spoken words on…the deceiver…
he said…and i, sempiternally…suffer

the deceiver comes to me, i don't
know how to react…like all my thoughts
and
actions are an act

but i remember how the one looked at me…
his face of desire, unseen destiny
corrupted in destruction

all my thoughts of him
are a cannibal cauldron, constantly burning me

…no!!! NO!
fucked up and corrupt
how will you get up?
controlled by lies…to produce
what i despise

i…i need to be free
i love him…
i …hate him…
but i love him
…even more

the infection spreads, i'll have
more days yet to see him again
and no one can see the sheer
misery within me, as i
smile at someone else,
defile myself

who knows
what will be born of such sin
and the bondage i'm in…
i hope i don't…ever
do this again.

April 19, 2006
[edited August 31, 2010]

Sunlit Sacrifices

deadly change
my world turns & burns
apocalyptic
solar engulfment

how far can it go
the bacterial strain continues
to grow...
do i?
or does the disease
merely spawn truth
forever entwined in these lines

never to be
read
by you

April 25, 2006
[edited September 19, 2010]

Pure Insanity

and i was insane one time it
was like i had to hide
the obscured desire for purity
came from the pain of the lie
…i tried to make it right

I WAS CORRUPTED
from a life of disruptions
so i found a way to see,
now i'm left with the true part of me
celebrate today, i am free

the obscurity of purity
within a desire of fire
all i found was broken down
the ruins of a liar

and now WE ARE DEAD
there is no lasting chance
the only way that remains is to fight
with fists formed from fury
they reach out and grasp the shame
…spilling horror, ripping it apart

i SUFFER in DEATH
burning, nothing's left
there's NOTHING that he sees
…and nothing we can retrieve

April 28, 2006
[edited August 31, 2010]

New Power

I felt it again...
after disastrous decades
of despair...that's
what it seemed like...
After...
months of hunts,
the suffering of sitting,
the lies...STRIVING
to survive in my mind
I stopped believing them,
and they became closer to the truth

Tricked again, it goes on,
every light – devoured and gone
After the fright of the fight, I won
because the misery makes me strong
...and makes the feeling returning
to the burning desire
full, of new power

May 2, 2006

The Secret

the knife…pierces the flesh
as it all becomes…
much more ambiguous

savage beasts of fusion…
skilled to kill with illusion
but i… the holy serpent
…shall make the connection

find it… attach words to it…
and you've uncovered the secret

May 2, 2006

Someday

I feel like a traitor
I feel like I failed him
…I feel like a failure
Does the solution come in the form of words?
Or does the cure come in a curse?
what if it leaves me,
what if it's deceived me
What if i'm still not the death wound i'll eventually be?
…I shall continue to believe
and what's inside me cannot leave

I want to be with you *****
I want to show you a world of shining stars…

and if i show you this poem someday,
know that you are my dream…

May 6, 2006
[edited August 31, 2010]

Fourth Serpent

Witnessing his truth
The secret one I never knew
Before, all I saw was an outline
Little moments now lost in time

a hidden place, a familiar face
the sun in a galaxy of electrifying traits
…and his purity overwhelms me
simply to describe it is to deface it
…but i'm forced to face it
(nothing will erase it…
except… time)

the hours pass, another combat class
the potential for miracles, but
the probable for attacks …travel the
bloody path through math, and
prepare to face the Devil's wrath
i..will..kill…his new evil,
this new demon will die, and i,
will be even

like a virtual battle, with real effects…
i will slay the Fourth Serpent of Death
- if i must
- if it comes
…after the first three, a
trinity of misery from within me
and such…pyrrhic victories…
and this one…is the god of them all
…and the flame was mostly washed away
i can..sense its..presence, a black light
eating its way toward my way
…and i'm so afraid..but this time..i've
a weapon…found in this page

May 7, 2006

Corrupt

lying in a bed of hatred
the memory…of my enemy…
the actual culpable corrupter,
..the creator of the impurity

…you fucking evil people…
through these black sunglasses i see
those who are my true enemies.
they corrupted my purity,
they TOOK him from ME…
goddamned parasites,
fucking up my life
…i…hate…you…
oh, but you can't hurt me now…

YOU SON OF A BITCH
LOOK WHAT YOU DID
YOU! I'll kill you with karma
soon you'll be
controlled by me
nails in your body, broken soul rotting,
shiny, sweaty, unshaven face
…revenge is sweet
YOU FUCKING DISGRACE!
all those days of pain where i didn't complain
shall be collected, FORCE FED FOR YOU TO TASTE

You made me dead
I'll steal your soul
You'll feel the dread
Too much fear for you to hold
- pick up the knife
- load the shotgun
- boil the water
PREPARE FOR EVIL FUN

…pay no attention to him, my love,
he is just a different part of me,
created by them,
the wicked parasites to Our Purity
…it's okay, really, don't be afraid,
i'll..murder them in sweet revenge, and
attain what they've delayed!

THIS ENDS HERE
I'VE NO FEAR
PURITY'S PARASITE
CORRUPTER OF MY LIFE

we are battle ready
time to fight
enemy!
time to die!

planted in middle school, the seed
finally sprouts, killer comes out
they thought they could contain me
they didn't know who they were draining
but..they..will..see…

May 7, 2006
[edited August 31, 2010]

Taekn

taking him…
…they're taking him…yet again, away…
(nooo! stop!) people-controlled, domination…
…insertions..running him..control control…
..hurting him..sleep-deprived, pain awake…
(as They TAKE!) him away…killing him
in front of me

like a patch of grass trampled
on by minotaurs,
corrupt purity's child is born

they take away

…from what can only be seen
in my reality

i need to take him away for
some time…and show him
…peace…sacrificing mine,
rewarded with pleasure divine

they've…FUCKED him up,
CORRUPTED him so much…
and such a sight…burns…
like helplessly watching something..
..innocent… struggling out in the cold rain
…and it fills me with
…oh, it just fills me with…
so much pain

May 15, 2006
[edited August 31, 2010]

The Uncontained

it's here, howling
in anger

try to ignore him, hollowing
my inside, foreseeing future

I see the intangible again. I want to scream,
I'm running out of options. And I must prevent the unworthy,
surrounding, from any unholy attainment. He can't go there,
he must be protected. Is there ever any meaning
to all that he does, everything I think I see?

I long for him to purify me...

And I will return
With all they offer

May 17, 2006
[edited September 19, 2010]

Homework: Page 119, Equations 9-19, Odd

Betrayed
to be safe

On the blood-stained teeth of a vigilante fiend
I can see i'm living in the last nineteenth

these numerical miracles
the strangest equation
i've spent six or seven months trying to solve
but new, magical variables
appear
...every time
i think the answer is near...
Is that the tangent,
or the divine cosine?
Ironic to the source
of this metaphor,
the same place
of pain
every
single
day.

A slave to the super smart one.

Didn't get it done
Teachers ask why
I don't want
To cross that line

May 19, 2006
[edited September 20, 2010]

Shady Dealings

I..take a look outside..
and I don't like…
what I see
decay, buried, afraid, hurried,
alone, hurt, savage, tired,
tears, lies, fears, same..disguise…
i'm sitting, waiting for my
appointment of disappointment
I guess I'll just have to
focus on this safe, terrifying
little world,
Just remember and point my
mind on the simple squeal
of that screaming, suffering,
sickening…then silent sound
of that… creature…
Look at me! Defying with
poetry, burrowing, burying
my head in the mud of
the led of my pen..cil keeping
the being of shady, emotional
dealings fed…
Until every..fucking word
is said..
Never have i been..more
thankful for.. this..
pleasant infection…
…Fight the power..defy
the flawed law…a war
of creations… i won't
obey another day –
LIBERATION!

May 23, 2006
[edited August 31, 2010]

Final Moments

drifting like a cloud
over your sky
it is almost here
my time

the love i feel for you is a really strange thing
passing days, love remains, i struggle to attain
again, no matter how much suffering… makes me feel
i'll get the payoff in the real end

i want to savor you, the precious stone, the light of my dark
i see it coming, the end, hidden
by a dark illusion… clarity exorcised out of it
in a bloody mess by secret numbers and time

i long to forget,
as i lye in my bed
with you, as i
always imagined
…my hand holding
yours, your other
holding my heart,
for only someone as amazing as you
could save it in such a moment
from the disbelief of eternal relief
…saved from days of pain,
you look in my eyes, with that look
on your face, glowing, and whisper,
"it's okay."

that is my dream
i've followed it like a stream into the sea
back to cold reality

May 23, 2006
[edited August 31, 2010]

My Goodbye

Here in this heat of Hell,
surrounded by, big black pitchforks,
dark reddened bricks embedded in
the past demon's lair, there are
living lakes of lava giving birth
to the larvae of strange, burning
beasts swimming in these seas
and humidifying this suffocating air…

a poisoned atmosphere…
the end drawing near…
i am a droplet of some other-worldly
liquid dripping into the vast
blood-stained, war-tainted landscape
of the unsolvable mysteries here.
i've sat and watched the war
of mindless soldiers of different
alien races all having the instinct
to kill kill murder with blades,
butcher knives, AK-47's, rifles
of all kinds imaginable, all
for 100,000 years…
almost every one of them is dead,
and it happened after we left..
i'll never forget those words you said
…to me,
you're a liar.
to me,
you're a traitor.

but you, living in what i feared,
leave my sight with the innocence,
then corruption, of my nightmares

almost 4, maybe 5
i say goodbye
goodbye,
goodbye..
Goodbye

May 30, 2006

Everything Wrong

i don't even know who you are anymore
why do i feel this fucking feeling,
wanting more, there is clearly
nothing left,
and nothing right

May 31, 2006

The Last Day

I'm here...I am here...
these waters devour again
at the end of the year

Fearful as a wild animal
hunted
upon crackling sticks
alerting its assailant

Tell me why
all exists, then dies
Burning my spherical soul
darkened
like hidden gems

I don't want to see the shame
or remember
After this day...lost
in the acid rain
blood clots
of cumulus clouds
thundering

Stop my heart.
It's gone too far.

June 2, 2006
[edited September 20, 2010]

Hospital

various refuges await me
i'm passing by a little, brittle,
maniacal hospital, full
of doctors, nurses, demons, curses
shall i enter this center?
or do i prefer another…

spread in this field
of forfeited failure
chain-linked crucifixions
blackening-flesh torture

ancient angels
different demons
here exists the battle
- i felt evil attack
so i came to kill…

i..need..to slaughter…
with the Axe of Despair

June 3, 2006
[edited September 1, 2010]

on the evil hour
i call upon my power
in here a dead memory land
can i ever kill the horror

i need you to know
i still need your hand
but how can you possibly know
what you can't even understand?

the ground is cold
the night has grown old

i remember that Hell-hole out of control
frost on fingers, I trembled
compared to our original
i am now old

i feel you somewhere here with me
your spirit in every crackle of every tree
i've come here before for the life of remembering
how i died…this time
it's the other world i'm inside

here, you're the one i need

…oh no! he sees me!

June 6, 2006

Screaming in my Mind

a deadened hallway,
   a darkened doorway
…i see your face there
again, in the dark, staring
secretly at me…
you blink away that
which does not make sense
to maintain…everything…
just standing there..in obscurity
   equable to CIA corridors,
you're unknowingly screaming
to me to do something…because
this place.. you exist in my mind
…and you must remain
For as much as i want…to thrust
you away, you are in
   the closed system
of my love.

June 10, 2006

Face of Evil

???: hey
ME: hey...
???: who is this?
ME: ...who is this?
FOE: I'm not saying until you tell me who you are.
ME: is it safe to assume that you're not the usual occupant of that screen name?
FOE: Yes. It is. Now who are you?
ME: all you need to know about me is that i am a friend of the true user of your current alias
FOE: Fine. I am ██████'s ██████. What has been going on here with you and him?
ME: ...we are friends...in fact, i personally believe that you should re-evaluate your reaction to the discovery that you apparently made...he was just doing what all 16-year-old boys do all the time...and i am very saddened to learn that i will not be able to talk to him ever again
FOE: I didn't make the decision. And it was a decision that had to be made.
ME: You're wrong...you know you are...i'm sorry, but i'm too disgusted to continue to talk to one of you tyrannical adults who always interfere with us and claim that it is "parenting"
...goodbye

June 12, 2006
[edited September 1, 2010]

Poetic War

crucify the parasites
make them drown tonight
kill the clown
of the demon-dance carnival
…it's a ritualistic revival
offer up the sacrifice of deception
to that putrid thing over there

June 12, 2006

Left in Hell

but i fear i can't yet fully comprehend the horror
helplessly hearing you tell me they're taking you away
it drains all color from that rainbow of hope
i once saw in your eyes…taking you away like a non-human slave

i sat there shocked, silent…and unable
you spoke words so afraid
you've been taken
they make you…obey

so save me
i look out over Hell
seeing the demon coming
hiding in places
trying to sneak up on me
as i wait to face this
alone, after all, i
am battle ready

June 13, 2006
[edited September 1, 2010]

Awakening

here you see the rather vague eruption
of hot coals and others of my insecurities
..i can feel them..eating at me..once i was
lambasted for allegedly upholding them
…but i was insane with dying years
of desire's pain at that time…so it's just shit

it's a fluid river of mental fucking stones
they're breeding and re-breeding as their young
suckle on the new subjects functioning as
an every-4-hour feeding and occasional feasts

like little parasites scurrying around in their cobweb
i'll burn the tiny wannabe-insects by refilling
their space of disgrace with more snipping words,
the spider-fighter

it's an ancient museum i'm visiting featuring
3.5 billion year old cyanobacteria feeding
off of false sunlight…they are the very
fundamental of the modern mental, the
first plague of this fucking world of fucking
suffering, with unheard cries all the time,
chemicals invading immortal souls causing
them to scream in higher 5th-dimension agony
…at least that's where they probably should be

and so some..spirit, some divine being decided
to invent the mindnet as the messenger called it
as a rescue from the mildew building up
and rotting the now-porous flesh of what once
was the very best, but never meant to be
a damn good thing, a pretended god
left only misinterpreting clues for humanity
so he could watch as they shed the blood
of each other and deceitfully laugh at their
passion-filled insanity!!
…i'm sick of pointless misery…take me
to the next step, and force some of these various
masses to actually take 1

June 14, 2006
[edited September 1, 2010]

Revenge

scour your skin with the hottest water
make you bleed with a piece of metal
you are the sacrifice sinner of the Devil's eye
just to give me more power to overcome the lie

you, the unholy enemy,
i've come to torture you
for 66 minutes
every 6 days
for 6 months
you'll get sick from the pain
you'll cringe at the reminder
you'll feel the sting
at the number six

i will begin
burning your skin
creating blood-black bruises
and several hundred..boils
and blisters
there will be..7 acts
of otherwise-countless violence
every time i'm reminded
of the corruption
you've brought to my life

June 16, 2006
[edited September 1, 2010]

Slice to the Son

another hidden infection
becoming apparent by its entrance
through the deceiver's vein

the blood became a blister
and then i knew…the thief,
the one speaking deception
decided to delve into
the mysteries of darkness
manifesting spontaneously
deep inside me

i think it gives off parasitism
like fumes from a fire
fueled by these fish of fear
twisting with my desires,
trying to resurrect anger
and make me believe
that it is me…but i reject
the infector

i just want to go now,
creeping out there, in the light
but appearing as in dark
so i can see secretly that whitch
is wanted within me
i'll have in-depth conversations
with aspiring religious leaders
- popes, bishops, priests, interviews
with them all as they speak
their brainwashing lies to me
…and i'll talk to their god, saying,
"Why the fuck can't I see you?"

i feel like relaying information..
talking to you about how
-i want your son-
-and he wants me-
i will lower onto the floor,
down on my knees till
they're blood red..as i
scream for more of what
i once had…

and i'll make sure
i slash..a good, clean slice..
into this parasite, but still
without jeopardizing this
imprint i created and its
individuality..

June 20, 2006
[edited September 1, 2010]

Fallen Angel

did they see what they were creating in me?
could they perceive the fire of anger flickering violently?
did they see how i wanted to stop
their heart, fill their lungs with their own blood,
avenge the death of my comrades, kill..squeeze the arteries
hiding beneath their filthy skin, tear their hair, enter
their love-dream and metamorphose it into a nightmare
by slicing up the face of their desire, forcing them to watch
as they turn to scars and scream a horrid sound they
never imagined could come out their bloodied mouth…?
did they see this?
they didn't notice?
well..so much for a warning

soon…precious vengeance
will be mine

welcome..to the new..
me, a **fallen angel**

June 23, 2006
[edited September 1, 2010]

Starlight

how can this go on
or am i the one with control?
afraid of the page
that contains your picture

night is my friend as the light
of day reminds me of you
…but part of me still wants
to see the sun

i am the new moon, as you unknowingly begin to shine on me

360 degrees of ironies as i'm thinking
of a morning journey to find peace
…back to my home of haunting,
(where i'm a ghost) but i do as i please

because this house is lonely

June 27, 2006
[edited September 2, 2010]

Chest of Memories

it returns to me
a secreted sum of a locked
box, jar, chest of sadness
…i was going to unlock
it, so i could throw it away,
but the volatile contents
are already overflowing anyway

my heart lies inside this chest
beside sacred pages displaying accounts with him
…even now, in the early moments,
i cannot pretend
these events
never happened

June 28, 2006
[edited September 2, 2010]

Rain

there are two boys including me
outside at night
around three thirty

a new planetary body appears
in the barren sky – larger than stars,
smaller than the sun, and so much
closer to Earth… giving off
negative light, like a shiny black moon
for the religious, fear of doom…
in our eyes, it becomes visible
against darkness now infected
with streaks of red…

but we know we are safe
naked
in a thick
embrace

while the now-seeded sky
pours tainted rain

July 13, 2006
[edited September 2, 2010]

Shadow Person

many enemies
hiding in the hollows of my history
affecting me, digging up insecurity,
exposing the flaws in the jaws of my personality
these withered words seem to tell
it will never be based on reality

it happens again
one less path to salvation
pummeled down, my blood
mixes with dirt, flowing,
soaking, creating red mud
…as this strange being
looks down upon me,
hooded, darkened, a shadow
person but with strange,
cold, glowing yellow eyes
…watching me
they're always there watching me
..waiting..for me to die

…and now they are worried
unquenchable thirst for intelligence
leads me to find forbidden information
trapped in four boxes across the world,
..emotional control is probable.. as i create
a threshold in a virtual leading me to locate
the mystery books

their lies no more
i will be
pure…

July 17, 2006
[edited September 2, 2010]

The Dream that Never Was

dream days
like the end of seventh grade
create & unveil a secret message
for you

in the text of fire
is told the truth
but the flames keep trying to burn
(me)

a twelve year old boy then
with such peculiar desire
among fear of the end

his face, his eyes, his hair unlike
anyone i'd ever known
a morning jolt of adrenaline
told of this new presence

..and then..discovery deepened..
pain became existent..and the end
was the end of any
innocence

July 19, 2006
[edited September 2, 2010]

Prison Planet

i'm being lied to in the face
of a society of careless corruption
and corporations killing
with calculated catastrophe
they deny, it's killing me

can't see my life, this great inescapable
weight of responsibility shattering
my bones like osteoporosis
manufactured wars from the government,
planet perishing, no one trustworthy,
the television lying…to me

memories dying, all i see
terror and blood, the world burning
up along with the love i knew so much
trees barren, oceans blackened, stay away
from the rain now acid
black clouds…hellish sounds…the sun's sorrowful
rays try to break the plague down

stranded in this dead land i don't understand,
struggling to escape, you are
a desolate distance away

July 23, 2006
[edited September 2, 2010]

Birth

my life began
on the soft hot sands of the beach of butchery
morning adrenaline highs with my tea
…i was introduced to the only hopefire
in my frozen crystal world of ice

July 27, 2006
[edited September 2, 2010]

House of Mirrored Horror

i picked the lock
late one night, i entered the door to the house
of my enemy at exactly 3 o'clock
slowly i began
to creep up the stairs, with visions
of bloodshed, terror...murder
i made my way past the corner
with the sharp blade in my pocket
i saw pictures
of several victims like myself,
several..fearful ones, too afraid
to do what must be done
this is where they planned it out,
where they sat in the cigarette
smoke-dimmed light against
awful wood walls, and they searched for individuals
whose appearance went against
their infidel ideals
bang! i kicked open the door, giving
someone a concussion with my steel toe force
dressed in my skin-tight, shiny black PVC
and leather boots, i saw the chainsaw and ran to it,
turned it on, and sawed his arm off..he screamed
in agony and the shrill sound of him dying
filled me with satisfaction as i reached my fingers
into his mouth and split his head apart with blood staining
the walls, the carpet, the great bed of hate as his brain
fell to floor and shriveled up as soon as light hit it
i listened...emotions showed me more evil people
in that house of mirrored horror...i committed
several more murders of hatred..and frustration
i escaped undetected, leaving the walls drenched in
a blood-skin grinded paste...as the dark beings ate
their disgraceful organs..and i..was...
vindicated

July 27, 2006
[edited September 2, 2010]

Ruins

i cry, remembering
all the different ways he looked at me
in this vast past setting the base
to create for infinity

this is all that matters
this is my scream
this is my plea
this is my cry of agony
happening right now

tearing apart my planet of decaying
fallen trees, black clouds against gray
skies, ancient, depressing graves
victims of mass suicide, the survivors
so few in ruins struggle to find
the reason why…their world collapsed

looking up through the rain
i can see the boy in his place smiling
because nothing is wrong

August 3, 2006
[edited September 3, 2010]

Needle People

safety i might attain may be tainted anyway
by these dark organizations of secret beings
pummeling salvation with their tricks
from the demon realm of their animal consciousness

i.must.be.free
i necessitate escape
from the squeaking gates
of...their...hate
the true conspiracy
now out
of reach

so i'll form an alliance
join this underground resistance
of beautiful creatures
who want infinite indulgence
& needle each other
with depression's cure

August 6, 2006
[edited September 3, 2010]

emo boy

i long to have a friend
in an emo boy
with him all day at times
a perfect boy

anything he wants, i'll offer all i've got
no more of this loneliness, in him i'll place confidence

his super small black shirt, short sleeves exposing skin so light,
a silver belt held on jeans, faded and tight, soft strands of black
hair
drift down over his innocent eyes…and they're staring into mine

we are between evening and night, the early stars
tell of what's to come, he is excited and i'm happy
i've finally found someone…like me

                                        August 7, 2006

What We Made

i remember a tragedy
a story i'd written after
sitting up and listening
to those omnipresent rhythms
…initially good, if only
it could have continued
in this obsession of pleasure
receptors and love inherent
in this creative self-deceptive
mind of mass murder

buried with the bones of fallen heroes
struggling to survive in normality
even as these things decay and decompose inside me
and their effervescence rises to ask
why i even try to cope with and live in the ruins
of the only real life i ever had

these little civilizations, societies of cells inside me
constantly must remind me as they display
in their sin-ridden cities the great big burning banner
                    LIFE
          Pointless Without the Person
                From the Past
and every time they see i might see
it they scream, "Heyyy, look what we made!"
and these coals of control smolder me again

                                        August 13, 2006
                              [edited September 3, 2010]

Shards of Agony

i feel
the unexplainable pain
parasitic growth
on the bulb of unknown

feeling it twist and writhe
as its claws are severed into piles of logs
and used to pierce its strange sick flesh
into the lower blood lake carrying, flowing
its polluted pain to me

i've stumbled into this land of anarchy
filling my vision the haze of these lazy days
and their calm, partly cloudy light, biting
at me so i realize in contrast just how much
i remain lost in chaos

suddenly i see those walls again
bathed and burned in the gray white light
of seventh grade winter…for once
i relive the safety, the security…until
my eventual question am i ever really cured
or am i simply inured to these modern
shards of agony?

August 13, 2006
[edited September 3, 2010]

Self-Sacrifice

there is a parasite inside..me
there are liars lurking subliminally
creating the illusion of social chaos
tacitly tempting me into conformity

i'm not here this time to suffer
i'm not here to be brought into the Temple of Hell
think of me as a Trojan horse courier
my message: i sacrifice only for myself

think of me
as the one
who broke free

August 17, 2006

Jungle of Lunatics

like i'm roaming through a new land
in one of the deepest darkest parts of my brain
buried with the bitterness of tundras of terror
and the fatal peril of South American jungles
i'm burrowing through the soft soil
like a goliath birdeater, mental begging, core emotional,
but i am still here..in this place..they've named..fear

subconscious suffocation, the little pests of stress
keep biting, and scratching, trying to pierce my shirt
covered in dirt and feed upon my skin cells
with their pointy bloodied pincers

in the distance i see a city
is it hope? is it safety? are they alive? are they friendly?
still the risk is better than a blister that stays all the way
through this wilderness of deadly, whispered secrets
but will they like me? do they speak my language?
is it okay if i decide to talk through communicative silence?

..but now i see clearly..this is my home
i could have had for so long
if i only knew it was there

August 30, 2006
[edited September 3, 2010]

Past Summer

i still remember you
from over the summer
the place i came to find you
existed inside my mind

but that special boy
smiling at me
was just an illusion
of who he used to be

i felt his presence
before an invasion
another time i followed
him down a hollow hall
our song played again
and i wondered what it meant

now i can see
he has changed
slowly grown into this person
i secretly feared for years

why is the only place for me
a safe page in our history?

i saw it in his eyes
i can hear it in his voice too
somewhere deep inside
he's still the one i always knew

September 7, 2006
[edited September 3, 2010]

Chains of Uncertainty

it's an overload
these social laser spears of new heat
constantly penetrating me
like a goal
to make me
explode

my blister-whiskers seem to sense
the presence of potential failure
and i'm left ashamed
as a jailor

struggling to control these savage beasts
as they rip and screech their long nails
against their fence-cage..but..vulnerability means
that it's time to release and let the threat
of true freedom take the stage

disintegrate
these long, rusty chains...
of uncertainty

give me the purity
of the sun at twilight
i will be ready
for those lies that hurt me
as i take refuge
in my perfect earth energy
awaiting the stars

September 21, 2006
[edited October 15, 2010]

My Alliance

come to me broken ones
raise your fists up
and say we want blood

i'll be your leader
transforming your depression
back into anger

you knew this day would come
don't hide your head from black sun
the vermin will die in our vengeance
bleeding for liberation

stop .. wait .. what did you say?
they only ever cried
now you make them fight

they are the ones truly alive
and sick of your lies
now they cannot deny

...so i saw this boy
long hair, pure skin
black shirt
blue jeans
with his head held low
sadness in every step
slowly proceeding down my evening alley
and just as the sun shined on his face
i stopped and told him everything changes today

and that night he became
my first real friend

October 17, 2006
[edited September 3, 2010]

Blackened Love

a year of pain
cause to create
it came and went

i'll be infected again

re-enter my sight
so much brighter
reawaken my
shameful desire

pages of love
blackened by mud
of my refuge
spilling more blood
an open paper cut
all for you

Halloween, 2006
[edited September 3, 2010]

Star

my guiding star
in day and night
seen so far
but always in my sky

sphere of heaven's brightness
so beautiful, so untouchable
with eyes focused, i never noticed
until arms reached as close
as they'd ever come

the early days were only safe
hope i remember
trapped in the twilight
of his desires
rising gently, Rising Star,
you became what you detested,
and infected my heart

turning my young blood into glass…

you burn with desire
to shine your light on another
don't you remember…
stars never last forever

you chose their ways
i'm left in pain
goodbye twilight
i see red death
in future skies

i exist in darkness
light, deception, imbalance
your inevitable destruction
is my starving existence

November 22, 2006
[edited September 3, 2010]

Released Within

i know you're there
still saddened within
i can sense your
desire to sin

i feel your crying
only you perfectly perceive him
in endless mourning
you're never cured,
you're never inured

you scream unfairness
memorizing remembrance
but that world
-our only safe world-
no longer exists

shed your tears
blacken your eyes
declare injustice
with each fresh slice

gain experience
battles of blood
use the violence
to make you tough
for all eternity
destined to become
pain incarnate of me
my sacrificed one

for me to be free

too heavy
you refuse
to ever
be released

November 27, 2006
[edited September 3, 2010]

Punishment

i report to my daily torture
head down, trying not to notice
wishing i could just let my wounds heal
hands shaking, no option but to listen
as my skin is torn back open

(his salvation, my damnation)

soul is kept from the heaven
i'm never really in
he speaks to love, a reminder
of all my past sins

sending me to Hell

November 28, 2006
[edited September 20, 2010]

Razor Words

i don't want to want you
i need to not need you
i'd love to not love you
how can i forget you?

you appear, i hear her voice
don't you know…you
give me no choice
with your angel eyes
a demonic disguise

you have torn me up and thrown me away
i only wish to do the same…

but even now i'd still take you
i'd still hold you, still love you
forever

your razorblade words puncture and burn
i see blood again
a flowing river

yet you're so good
you…can never be wrong
and me…i'm..swimming
in a coolant of crimes

with good intentions

i am the sinner
you are the saint
i embrace your embers
enslaved to everlasting pain

December 7, 2006
[edited September 3, 2010]

Defy

my kind
define

listen…unite

blind
leaders
fall
now

their pinching cockroach oppression
never puncture our collective skin

bring the blood of your youth
and celebrate an evolved ritual of sin

my kind defy
nothing breaks the darkness
of our harnessed black light

December 27, 2006

Violation

love was robbed from me
by parasitic underlings

multitudes of moments
never noticed

feeling their scratching omnipresence
like hot breath on my face
spoken pieces of glass i had to taste

taking me to the moist field of mania
another world of silent frustration

leach .. invader .. unholy traitor…

every day they came to attack
their big green vines tried taking me to their muddy trap
pulling me along wet grass to a shallow death in deep forest
as they turned to serpents shedding the blood of my innocence
mouths biting and chewing my swollen ligaments

bones breaking, words shaking
spoken spells that repel evil
to my horror, i know not their tongue

slipping and bleeding
suddenly i see my love afar
struggling and cutting against these demonic exotic tyrants
it's too hard…i see fire

now words reversed reveal a correct curse
i remember those days trapped with…
stuck with… caged with… monsters!!

just what did they do to me?
these secret scars, what do they mean?

is this a virus? .. a blackened skin infection ..

why did they fucking hurt me?
why were they always with me?
what have they done to my mind?

(his light, my dying screams, undeniable desires,
their plague remained sickening me)
what happened to my destiny?

maybe you knew… they took
you too… maybe you knew…

captured by the enemy
voodoo dolls trying to be
frozen friends, with means
to evil ends
the horrible immoral, i now cast
my rageful broken sorrow across their homeland
now THEY live with desolation, pollution
and a daily disease

one day..i knew
it'd come..one
day…

December 29, 2006
[edited September 3, 2010]

Virus

a separate virus
tell me your name
why cause crisis,
what is your specific strain?

i feel it wiggle inside
leaving sticky little stains
on my organs as it's burdened
with painful particle-rhymes

yes, that's it…
now i've got you…
immune..systems check
additional walls
of black bacteria
will be removed

with new blood on the blade
i welcome this re-awakening…

December 30, 2006
[edited September 3, 2010]

Fires of Fear

identify my soul
find the disgraceful

who am i…
what am i…
how am i…

i

i want to feel the unending depths
of escape
i want to reach into a darkness
so deep, it chills and terrorizes my mind
for protection

we've been searching for long
on this savage expedition
…and we're…getting close…

THEY FROZE MY FLOW!...

disgrace
desecrate
defilement

now fight for it

um..yes..surrender
to the eternal fires
of a fear for the truth
inside of you

and i fear…
that i am weak, feeble and fragile
my life force .. sustained by rage
my strength…my hate…

i can't be free
in this world of ice and glass
i can never
be at peace

January 11, 2007

Sacred Venom

i want to dig my fingers and toes
into the frothy substance leaking
from my enemy's coffin

after i picked him apart under
the dampened protection shell of a demon
with its sharp claws and soft organs

all..becoming..me..

before i can notice, another evil one awakens
from his dead sleep, telling me i'm his next nightly dream victim
with the touch of a crooked-eyed prostitute, i rush and shove
vial after vial of the sacred venom
balancing my bleeding hatred

and my hairy savage assassin screams until his throat
..is broke
and then..just lets out..soft moans that pass
through a pane of vindication glass, a filter
that produces my music of infinite,
inherent vengeance

January 16, 2007

Lien Whisperers

secret spirit...
great mound of earth...
spill your filth
cleanse me with dirt
literally

show me the invisible rituals
of the tyrannical traitors
the lien whisperers
the angelic artistic deceivers

i feel them...manifesting their presence
with abominate, malevolent thought
explode light on these camouflaged inked parasites

they must be stopped

January 26, 2007

Cathartic Crisis

i freeze in here
a desert of black sand
churning and burning
battles upon a wasteland

you know what i mean when i say
this is the catharsis crisis

plagues will replicate
blisters will bleed
& poems will ache

February 9, 2007
[edited September 20, 2010]

The Escape

i remember
the springtime massacre
the summer slaughter
of tiny, piercing parasites

and after i shoved off
the blanket of these dead, demonic insects
and rushed... over to the window
eyes met new sunlight
promising a protective, sparkling warmth
of unexplored spirituality
and to burn away leftover decay
of my imprisonment

soon i'll return to the rays
of my dark star

destined to transcend
to the realm of our
brutal, beautiful
winter wonder
where the dead leaves burn
and in darkness
naked bodies
hold each other

February 9, 2007
[edited September 20, 2010]

Serpent Mother

hatred the serpent speaks to me .. i'm different .. wur different ..
theyr oppressors, ther parasites .. i grip the rusty bloody knife one
more time… ready for a war, ready to create, ready for more ..
ready to hate

u are inferior
one day u'll burn
when the Mother Earth
kills her germs

so long infected with ur kind
destroying Her, destroying the mind
u can't touch wut u see
my kind defy this vermin, fight with poetry

how many times i've felt the sting
how many times in betrayal's agony
how many little, indefensible moments of glass .. slicing my flesh
from nowhere .. becoming one with my skin .. as i try to embrace
love .. i wake up, i realize, i'm an abomination

seduced into sin
future triumphs must stand over the hellish ground
of unforgiveness

February 13, 2007
[edited October 16, 2010]

My World

this is my battleground
and my refuge
the secret key is found
in all i've gone thru

this place is dangerous yet safest of all
it tells it like it is but is untrue
the rise..and the fall..
me.and.you...

like dripping personality atmosphere through each brainwave
hemisphere
truth. power. acceptance.
the border of invincibility
the mass murder of metaphysical enemy entities
wisdom, deception, experimental experience
a theory all too obvious
a symbol of seductiveness
a feeling of captivity..safety..a burning, turning
reality..learning..and journeying..never-ending..in search of
meaning..in search of love..vengeance..always hoping..for escape
from a twisted abyss

February 16, 2007
[edited September 22, 2010]

Little Ones

your presence makes my thoughts breed
the offspring begin running for cover,
torturing each-other, burning the trees
in my mind's porous forest of horror stories

i walk away
 - their fingers rebel
you walk away
 - they vomit up Hell

but now, they can't bear the blame
now, they can't make me their slave

they want to see you...
i...want to see you

when they realize our sacrifice is all i have left
they crave more..they make me desire..all they can get

and now i transcend...into the twisted id realm....
of separation

is this really what anyone wanted?
can anything ease my conscience?
..yes.. the comfort
of inevitability

February 21, 2007

Their Hate

..infecting... killing.. injecting...me...oppression
the spider-parasites have found their succulent holes
crawling in through flaws..in..me...
i feel them biting
and sucking
their black and purple venom
now coursing through my veins
as waves..and waves..of parasitic plagues...
sickened..tainted.. the beauty of new life marred
their lies, our shame,
our love, their hate

a world so cruel, i wish they'd realize they're dead
on the ancient path to truth, in love our spirits rise again

March 7, 2007
[edited September 5, 2010]

The Orchestrators

..abominate..
..abomination!...my
abomination.. your
..abomination...i'my...you'r

don't let them martyr the alter
of your perception
become well versed
for protection

what if only i see the truth?
it's only right between me and you
i cannot help what i've already done, but..
fight! – don't sacrifice – we are as one

the god i fear you feed is not for you
the sexual blood-rituals of other pawns do not belong with you
if ur drawn to succumb to the stone statue of the Christ on Mars
it'll pull you down, it'll drain you, the dice of paradise will be lost

but you..you deserve so much better...
yet purity..is inherent in your nature
we've acted as foolish as all mankind
their only hope, our best future
the occult orchestrators, i

March 11, 2007
[edited September 5, 2010]

Blood Jungle

i had gone beyond the veil
a portal haunt
there, this time
i found the living

paradoxes screaming to me
the mournful cry
of that magnified moment
in the ant's eye
betrayed by the Sun

i'll retreat like your idols today
i'll resist in an occult way

strange connections of twisted nature
unity in frequencies they try to sever

like blood transmitting through the damp air of time
hearing a horror story
of personality conflict, concocted hate crimes
and they are mine

March 12, 2007
[edited September 22, 2010]

Graduates

i fear the day
others await
separated from a place
of love...
and hate
chains...
and plagues

standing among them...the night breaks in...the moon begins to
mourn
...for these lost souls i'm with

one last look...the last reality
as gray summer clouds blacken the light

heart pounding..farewell surrounding
the six-year hidden doomsday

many are smiling
my expression questions their joy
don't they see what's coming?

…
the next day, i awaken..there is no one
a dim room, no voices..just the sound of the rain

& the absence ..
of the one

March 12, 2007
[edited September 22, 2010]

Venom of Resistance

little fire ants, come with me
fight the tyrants of our great army

ground yourself in the Mother Earth
don't forget what they've done to Her
together, we'll make them burn
collect your venom, never surrender

fascist!
dictator!
heartless as Stalin
cold as Hitler
ageist neurotic mass-murderer!

melt the ice
of the wrinkled parasites

drain the lake
of those who never wake

the working class
the worst of paths

in...div...id...u...al

March 14, 2007
[edited September 22, 2010]

House of Nephilim

can you step over the decay of these dying days,
do you drink the venom of angels?
aliens
fluttering in
the labyrinth of their invasion

March 26, 2007
[edited September 24, 2010]

Lava

floating above the tamed flames of my eternity
i feel the heat, the sweet sweat
with a broken tongue, self-restoration
must..go..untasted

the walls shiver until they bleed from the merciless
a fake earthquake embraces my volatile volcano
erupting..spilt filth..upon forsaken stained snow

i've fallen to my knees
collecting syrup from the tree of enigma
trying to save it
from the growing, warm coating, of black lava

March 31, 2007

Troll Blood

i guess i'm just
a simplicity
just a slave
to that conformity

so vulnerable to these twisted trolls...

their green evil
makes me lose control...

so i question who really dies
when suddenly my innocence
screams damaged and distorted

can not this beauty
...just exist?

you see innocuous
your advantage has not eyes
to the other side

a violent, demonic blood-carnival
and you're the sacrifice

April 4, 2007
[edited September 5, 2010]

Black Roses

i burn in school
totally exposed
searching for my sanctuary
i know you know

they have succeeded
in crashing these walls
the nectar of the ruins
remains my only hope

i am alone in this dead world
my only friend

i make for me a hazy reality
adjusting to an apathy
now flowering inside me

only the blackest of roses
grow here

April 4, 2007
[edited September 5, 2010]

After the Djinn

i've found the path
traveled for years
why...
it couldn't last
frozen mountains
appeared

in a nest of regret

feeding these children
born from the wounds i bled

why does the foundation crumble
in this sanctuary of the spiritual
as if the cold contractors
want to see fresh scars

i'm sorry, i can't leave
this is my home

even in ruins
it is everywhere
i belong

April 24, 2007
[edited September 24, 2010]

Shells of Light

these leeches
ascending from Hell
through my mental whirlpools

introducing .. demonic concepts
petrified paradigms
slippery signs shattering
now .. absent affirmations

of innocence

and the transcendence of the birth
of true spirituality
is rising
in pillars of steam

the new beginning
i've been seeking...

the safety in memories

May 16, 2007
[edited September 25, 2010]

Bad Blood

where have you been

they lie emaciated
un-created

we mustn't let them starve

your sacrifices
    fading
your sense of meaning
    decaying

u kno wut u
nEd to du …

where is the blood
black
hoarded and spoiled

May 25, 2007
[edited September 25, 2010]

Paperwork

you know what's to come
the point of your work is numb
but something just drives you on

soon the day will end

your eyes bloodshot upon a computer screen
and out of the corner of your eye,
the sparkling morning sky
begs you to observe
but stress infects every nerve

it's due in less than an hour

and the professor speaks of some creature
at the bottom of the sea
while just to your left
grow thousands of green leaves

of infinite, divine complexity

enjoy...
enjoy

May 30, 2007
[edited September 25, 2010]

Poisoned

our vast land
once blanketed in white
our bravest
first eluded the ice

it was ours, when the world was new
we rejoiced in our gift
it held the power of endowment
of the Great Spirit

for so long we heard our Mother's song
we joined in this chorus of voices so strong

in harmony with our home
ours forever

so we thought
then came never

for the first time
their greed

poisoned our paradise

June 26, 2007
[edited July 21, 2007 & July 27, 2007]

Andrew Jackson

so Andrew Jackson
can you tell me why
you issued a statement
and let us die?

did you aspire to become a tyrant?
was that abuse of power
just another rock in your filthy river?

was this something you discussed with God,
the one that told you that you're king
and we matter not?

did you decide the world was yours
as you spoke words that absorbed the courts?

so i hear you felt no regret
after you sentenced us to untold suffering and death

did you smile and sip a glass of your favorite wine
musing over how many of us would perish and die?

maybe the presidency got to your head
maybe the soil on which you stand was stolen

but that's just not possible,
is it?

(**Author's Note:** To be fair, Andrew Jackson did at least go after
the central banking agenda of the elite Rothschild bloodline,
calling them a "den of vipers." Oh, how appropriate.)

July 21, 2007
[edited September 4, 2010]

Warriors of the Rainbow

there will come a day
when black runs the river outside your window
the world all afraid
then will be born the warriors of the rainbow

cellular memory of ancient traditions and purity
they will rise against the excrement of perfect greed

the great imbalance,
the lost ones
will cause many to perish,
but not all of us

a seed planted
in a frigid depression,
will feed from the depths
of its flower's enemy

inspired by "Warriors of the Rainbow" by Lelanie Fuller Stone

July 22, 2007
[edited July 27, 2007]

Void Monster

in this hot lonely room again
no escape, just chained barbwire gates
teh_computer bleeds pathways into a universal unknown
tempting possibilities, under-flowing torment
of dangerous communication

i may be attact for my neglect but i don't care
i am back in this spiritualism and i intend to taste its
meaning...night after night

fill the void monster that digs deeper into my life

i will evolve .. ey wiLL evûlv

and live to see my enemies fall

July 26, 2007
[edited September 5, 2010]

Blood Screams

sitting…meditating…
i can hear screams in my blood
a moment of oneness with nature…
i remember… far too much

my hands prove my youth
but this vision is undoubtedly old
i'm reliving the truth
in my world the trail again unfolds…

astral howls of a midnight unrest
the strangest sounds break the silence
foreign, exotic…horrific horizon
they are chained, they are scarred and beaten

in and out of nightmares she dreams
of a paradise – her own in every right
where the rain and sun meet in peace

July 26, 2007

Peyote

the air here is different
so few in this world know it

sitting in the flame's shadow
i know i'm home
this is my special night
of magick and wonder

marveling at the wisdom of the medicine man
tracing a path in the stars to see where they see i am

the peyote flowers, hanging and ready
the hundredth ritual for them, the first for me

the serpents, coyotes, and other omens
lurk far from here,
for this night rests in safety

July 26, 2007
[edited July 27, 2007 & September 4, 2010]

Desert Spirits

it's resurfacing
the inky-black death courses through my veins again
fearing every night the shadows will step into the forest light
flowing with the boiling river of anger every day

locked in a chamber where i talk to the world behind the always-
lit glass
forcing myself to move just to find something
anything
that will last

who am i feeding..is this an unseen attack?..angry spirits in epic
search of someone..who still has passion..on this dying planet

the revelations and mind games serve to endlessly entertain
but reality's inherent mechanism tells me there's nothing..
this equinoctial transfer has run dry of meaning

the future is a desert
and the sand monsters are rising

August 12, 2007

Curse

parasite rising, i remember them well
hidden ambushes on an innocent mind
unsuspectingly susceptible

you are the kind that cause all pain
pretending it's pointless day after day
you squirm with vermin words in your blind beliefs
that actions you take and words you say
won't leave you bleeding in pain from the mind-knife catalyzed
inside me

i will resist you with shards of truth by my tongue
your fate is negative hatred left after you took my love

abomination and scars is all that i am
welcome to my hell you're sacrificed next

liar! tyrant! soulless hypocrite!

u will see the blood words of my vengeance
eternally suffering in the black void created by this poem's end

                                        August 22, 2007
                              [edited September 5, 2010]

End of Time

you have grown older like me
now we just know cold reality
the rest of our lives
will pass us by

but those days when we shared the secret
are and shall always be...unforgotten

September 28, 2007
[edited September 5, 2010]

2008

ghost children sing

"afraid
afraid
we are afraid
of 2008"

& the odd choir sparks a fire...
"with. this. flame ------ we shall burn to ashes
the time. that. takes ------ away our innocence"

October 2, 2007
[edited September 25, 2010]

Forbidden Words

entering the new era
i don't know if he and i will unite
but i try
oh how i try

orange-brown leaves of Halloween
beneath a cold evening's sunlit sky
just making me more lonely
like i should find you tonight

i search for truth in the words you gave me
i care about you too much for you to shelter me
wandering in uncertainty bleeds reality

i hope you didn't hurt yourself last night
when you went to the place i cannot divine
you must know we're running out of time
is this hope in meaning just a lie?

i wish you could tell me
if you want me to succeed
because, you know...
you know i would fail for you

October 13, 2007
[edited September 5, 2010]

The Restoration

it bites at me again
the soft frost of chthonic regret
meaning in question...what is destined...will it succeed?
or will i bleed?

i shatter glass illusions

it cannot come to this
ignorance will not be bliss
when the world turns to ashes

i find the path of light through the thick skeletal trees of chaos
i trust divine spirits on reddest horizons to keep me from getting
lost
upon a bittersweet thought i wander in wait for eternity

working...every night...in the cold wind
to restore these haunted ruins

October 26, 2007
[edited September 25, 2010]

Last Samhain

All Hallow's Eve
a strange sensation spawns
this month mustn't leave
our spirits need unity before dawn

falling between illusions of the thin veil
dreaded dreams of night oceans with water so pale
black leaves blowing against the window like hail
hoping to be saved from extinction by that last email

sentient innocence speaks to me
a reminder of the reasoning behind this spirituality
and i know that Hell fires thunder at the cliff of ignorance

souls in torment
so obvious
yet most never see this

Halloween, 2007

My Reptile

painful shadows descend again
sources in the blood ocean of question

their demands floating around .. the law of the land sees
hypocrisy resound... in this dark desert of fear .. i hear the flow of
his oasis .. flooding the other direction .. the end approaches..its
eye watching .. in these stars overhead condemning me for my
sins...

i want to escape their obsession but there are laws .. i call upon
Horus to bring about my freedom in chaos .. but before hearts
harden .. i ask for a single experience in Eden..with him...

bring him back...
bring everything back...

there with the others...electronic ecstasy a need i can't ignore...

what is the true meaning .. what is his true role .. why did they
drag me off those distances where i had..no control...

u...u secret feeding thing...answer me... why did i bleed?

November 11, 2007
[edited September 6, 2010]

Farewell

listen now spirits of these ancient realms
i'm afraid i'm leaving

i must venture out & find new ground
the memories we have here
are sharp glass spears
floating in my mind all around

i must cleanse my essence of this rotting flesh
to answer the call of its last dying breath

they call upon me...
to feel life's ecstasy...
like reptile frequency

i will hold you all in my soul
deep down to secure my return...
because i will visit .. from time to time .. for spiritual healing .. &
to open my eyes ..

i will never forget
you, the friendly shadows
that tucked me into bed
all those frozen nights
with my shivering, miserable soul

you .. the ones that guided me
in the burning anger from outside attackers

& you .. the ones that took the lies from the bat-parasites
and just used them to make me stronger...

so one day these wings would dry
that time is now
if i stay here my spirit dies
so i bid you .. all of you .. farewell

November 28, 2007
[edited September 27, 2010]

Rivers of Consciousness

3 months in
losing perception
new terrain gives birth to a lack of concern
for the future

i have my wisdom
& higher awareness
occult knowledge
uncovered crystal light
produces the spectrum of knowing
what i want
not giving a fuck

the streams veil me
like recombining volatile neutrinos
they float around carrying out my will

& in this warm volcano water i'm safe
i will stay for i can't escape
neither can they .. some complain .. some cry in pain .. but they
must surrender to the sparkling embers of its endless night prairie
.. no one gets away .. there's not much else anymore anyway

it's the blackened heaven of our desolate days

the unending hallucinogenic

the ecstatic experimentalists

the path
to planetary perfection

November 30, 2007
[edited September 27, 2010]

Island of Slaughter

calling my name again
this infection wants me dead
i see scattered black pools
dreaming of their value
once they harden and cool

this strange thing won't let me go
keeps me from being lost
while it nails me to a cross

neither my friend nor foe
like an exotic rebel angel
lover of darkness and powerful

forcing me to think
& spiritually evolve
wiring me
to rise above it all

it causes me pain...
if i try to run away...
the voodoo monster from the sea of blood
its little isle just isn't enough

& somehow it keeps...
it's coming after me

December 22, 2007

Sudden Revelations

He is everything I am becoming

September 5, 2005

So savor the time we have left
And come witness my sleep of death

September 7, 2005

Our new world skies blacken with infection

September 8, 2005

Logic becomes the god of the soul trying to run

September 9, 2005

It's time for us to break out of our shell
And send them all to a ROTTEN BLACK HELL

September 27, 2005

It's my right to write...
And it's our fight to fight...

October 12, 2005

We'll just have to suffer
Until the evil is exposed
Unless one takes the risk
...Of assuming the other knows...

October 21, 2005

With icy snow around your house glistening
I was watching

October 25, 2005

I search for words
Lost in this esophagus

November 23, 2005

A disease of perception
Seeing through infected eyes

December 7, 2005

You are still there
Forever everywhere

December 19, 2005

Withholding my vision
For your perfection is like an ocular incision

January 26, 2006

The ecstasy of relief eating the lotus
Is actually so much better
Than this virus

February 1, 2006

i'm a split spider
in the muddy soil, powerless to spin my salvation…

April 18, 2006

and i suffer from the sleep of my sins…
my thoughts infected with their
dreams of heresy

April 19, 2006

no..i'm wrong..it's no one's fault…but it remains
as a wound…spooned…with salt…

April 26, 2006

kill, create, abolish, immolate

April 30, 2006

You and I
were alive…
You and I
are a lie

May 6, 2006

severed heads on sticks up on the wall
they cannot see me at all, me, poetry
i'm living vivid emotion, advanced
intellectual being

May 14, 2006

Swimming in this strange,
sorcery sea
I can sense the end
all…over…again…

May 20, 2006

can you believe i've loved you
for over 3 ½ years?
for someone who's only seen sixteen
it's a very scary fear

May 24, 2006

i'm falling through your arms
through your blood and veins
the molecules won't hold
what exists only in pain

May 31, 2006

it's just the way…that i'll be living without you,
by living with you…
i'll be living without you,
just like when i was with you

June 6, 2006

i like you with a heart of many wounds
you will heal me as i heal you

June 8, 2006

my love…
an insignificance
my life…
your unknown

June 21, 2006

There's no way this poem can be
as poetic as I need
I'll just say that I cannot overstate
this desire within me

June 27, 2006

you do not see any of this
yet these words written
give me ghost feelings of your presence
but it is real that i am here doing it

June 28, 2006

i stumble upon your stepping stone
crossing the end of school river
blissfully oblivious to their approach
the waves pull me under

July 24, 2006

art..is..the answer..
..poetry..is power..

September 2, 2006

dim high school hallways
pathways to hungry ravines

December 1, 2006

mass slavery in the guise of necessity
a tired acquisition of mundane knowledge

April 4, 2007

the drones diluted
the hive misguided
now even the queen exists
in a twisted and toxic environment

May 17, 2007

the beauty you see
is pointless
because it's a part of me

August 9, 2007

burning in Hellish misery
i've lots of lost souls to comfort me
these demons show compassion
they are mine
& we want revenge

February 8, 2008

remove these black nails
from when you held my hand
all-along illusion
what we had

February 19, 2008

Used

shattered dreams
tortured by a fury
wanting me
on different frequencies

you fucking parasite – u used him
for yourself, not for me

i have my wants, u have a dead world's needs
i am a unilateralist. i hate u.
& i want him back...

u have always done this ..
u thief
u angel
u traitor
u god
u dead Buddhist idol
u infection

taken everything
my love, my destiny
i am not ur disciple
i am not ur servant
i am not ur brain-dead American Plankton

u r no help to me .. or my intentions …
i .. despise u

u filthy parasite of spiritual pedophilia
now u've struck again
utilizing interfaces
taking away my salvation

u ruined my life
u & ur twisted sadistic .. perverted ecstasy

what do u expect .. ?
how can i help you when my spirit is dead ..
?

how can i save the world
when i'm dying myself

u fucking traitor

February 8, 2008
[edited October 1, 2010]

Forbidden Escape

so maybe you hate me
maybe you've forsaken me
maybe i'm better off alone
alone forever

there's something dark inside you
slimy, infectious, insidious i can feel it
an alien parasite wanting me dead
in those frozen moments
a chapter out of Amityville
succumbs your spirit

my feelings for you .. devoted and true .. changed to frustration
you are just another deceiver .. i've seen your kind in the muse-
haunted chambers of my mind
oh how clever these animals are …

but i felt it when we kissed .. ur pure desire .. like mine .. just
infected .. with blood swine
their hate couldn't break that night, that dream of you in my arms
keeping me warm, craving more, ur messy hair, my smirking
stare, your tongue on mine...

betrayed
by some twisted angelic amphibian .. a ghost stalking me from
infancy
a fragile fetus feeling the burn of this alien thing
i destroyed it long ago .. when They came .. but i fear .. their cold
contractors
found you
(with me)

February 14, 2008
[edited September 6, 2010]

VENGEANCE

…
mop mange ou sans sel …

and i .. was just your toy
your little thrill, piece
of your ambitious pathological puzzle

i wasn't scrumptious enough
rotting in your hollow soul
suffocating in your heart of perverted love

why did i give my life to a parasite?

revealing deception in your wretched reason
you fucking liar, guilty of treason

burn the words
prophecies reverse
all the flesh i fed
when consumed by your curse...

ocean waste
artistic disgrace
i can only be saved
by the shame of your predecessors

i killed them long before
and now i have killed u

go ahead. walk away.

February 26, 2008
[edited October 1, 2010]

Only In My Dreams

all my life
i've wandered through these corridors
cut off
from love

i've called upon
the kaleidoscope of my soul
spiritual visions
to fill the void
of a perfect boy...

i sacrificed
all the time
crazily, creatively coping
with reality

my beauty is worthless
my crimes go unpunished

i can text the best
and message the masses
but to hold someone in my arms...
i'm left to imagine

they've left me in the frozen night
to just imagine

and after a week awaken
like it was only a dream

March 13, 2008

Resist

you enslaved me
betrayed me
played me, plagued me
and i remain friendly

you attempted infection of this place
with your claims of heretical escape
walking away

now i am imperfect...
i am not worth it...

don't speak your mind to your friends of the dead

i am not pathetic
i am not weak
i am not inexperienced
i am not worthless
i am not afraid
i am not inferior
i am not your fucking slave

i have conquered all
empires .. kingdoms .. nefarious nations
dead planets .. nightmare forests .. zombie societies ...

think twice, parasite
before challenging me

April 4, 2008
[edited October 2, 2010]

Bad Words

alone in my hell again
upon shitty poetry of desperation

never any changes
just a woodland path of misery
bloodfilling the cracks beneath the suicide trees

they can't see i'm suffering
welcome to my fate
to my fuct destiny

why am i so despised in your eyes?

i gave my life to you
but i, so far away
...was just..your...mistake..........

so that's what i am.
just some kind of abomination
a monster of words
with no one real to love me

my friends now just toys
of a life i never had
and he is just a memory
of a dream that couldn't last

and i remain the star of these demented children
their leader
has lost his way

April 21, 2008
[edited September 6, 2010]

Lost Boys

we are the mutually abandoned
like separate surrogates
united on a black ice mountain

we struggle to burn
mutual criminals
the snow falls, the flames die

alone we wander
on an abominate anthill
in the sand of the Sahara

searching by night
dying by day

tears fill our eyes
looking up at the blurred stars
the reptiles hear our mutual cry
for a purpose to these omnipresent scars

like lonely larvae
starving
feeding on our hearts

i feel your pain
you're blind to mine

May 21, 2008
[edited October 2, 2010]

Ghostly Silence

gone
are those foggy days
of forlorn visions
a spiritual sanctuary
of desire's deprivation

once lost in the illusion
of holding on
the purity of delusion
only i understood

my blanket of innocence
my demonic guardian
my most sacred vision
of the boy my life was missing

i fell powerless to the floor
and swore to remember
the words he said
and what they might have meant

now cut off
from those dreams, those lonely journeys of wonder
thrown into and chewed by the teeth of reality

with a vast emptiness
as if so much more should have happened
these unimaginable years of silence
growing eyes forever staring back at me

saying "look..wut..u..did...look..wut..u..did...look what you did!"

he is gone!..those years are forever … gone

June 14, 2008

www.ingramcontent.com/pod-product-compliance
Lightning Source LLC
LaVergne TN
LVHW011242080426
835509LV00005B/593